FUNNY PET

GRAYSCALE COLORING BOOKS

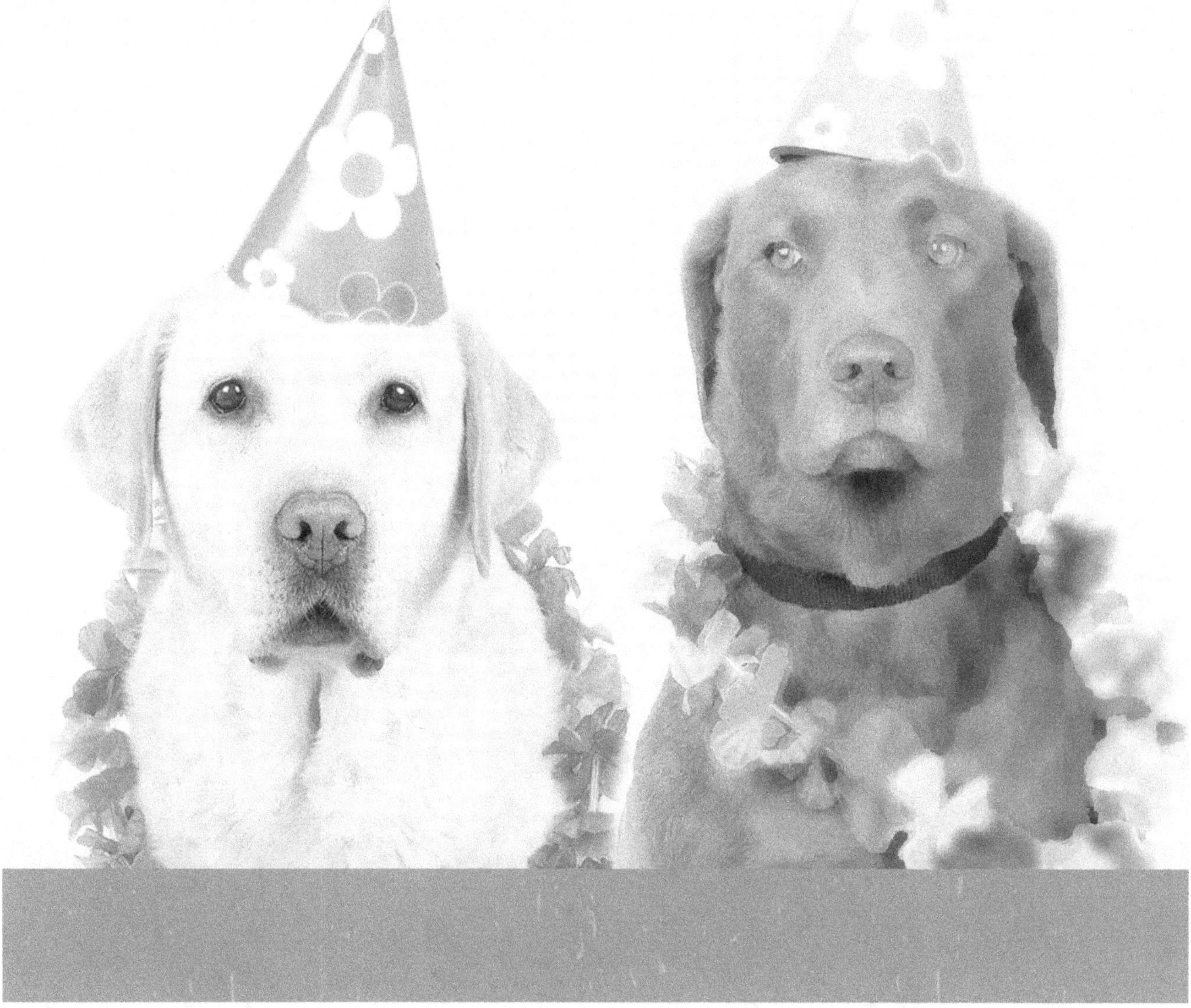

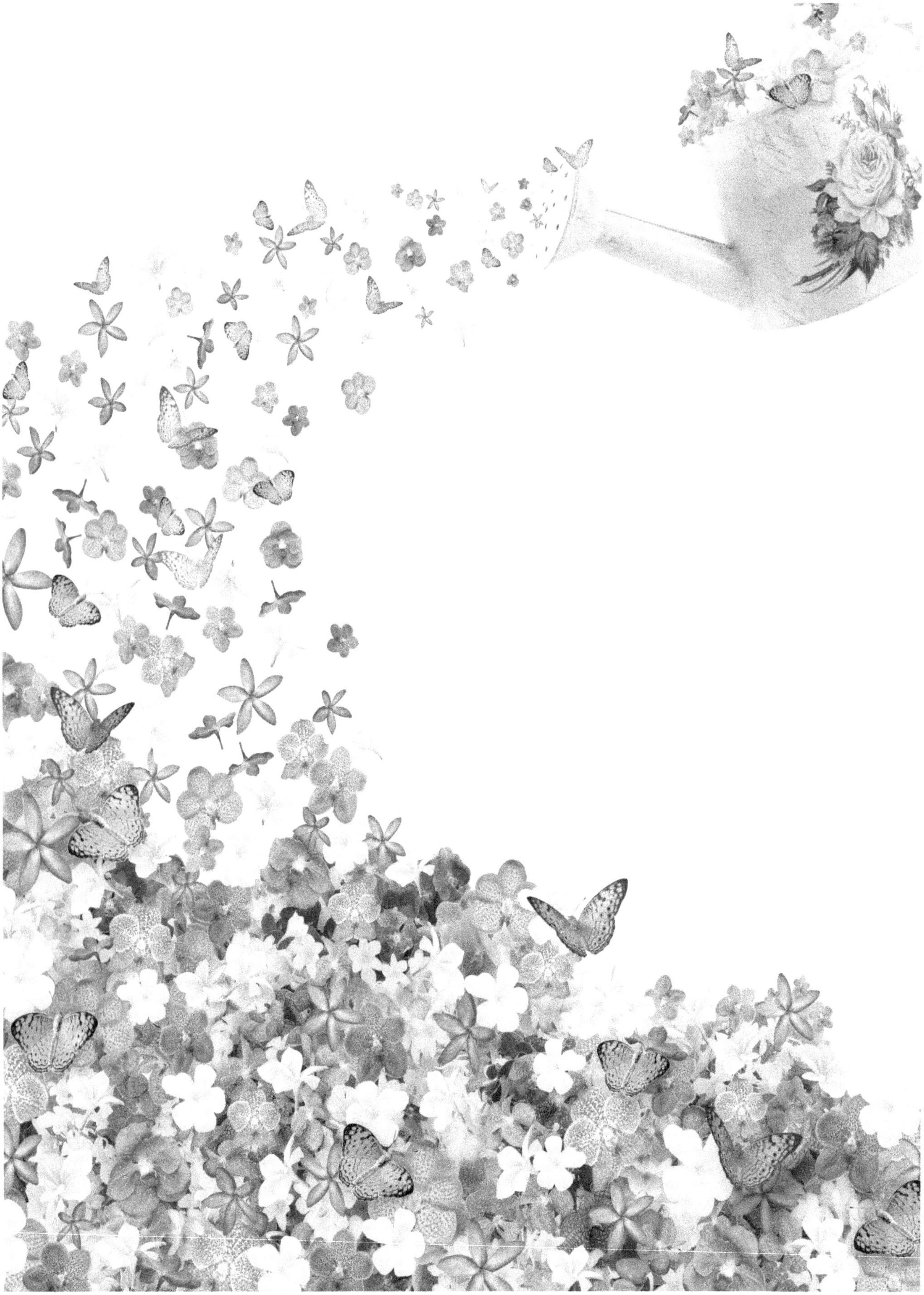

COLOR TEST PAGE

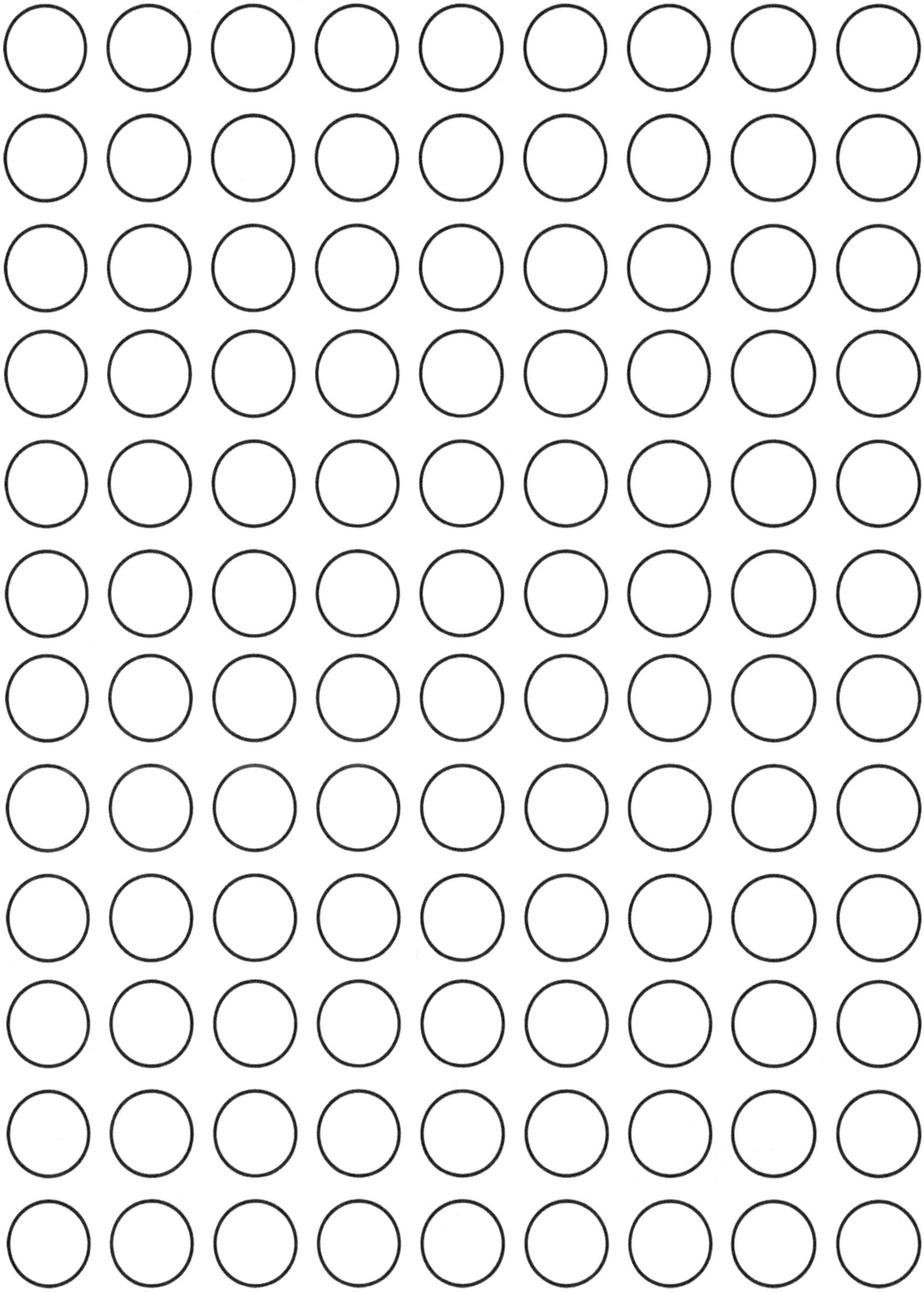

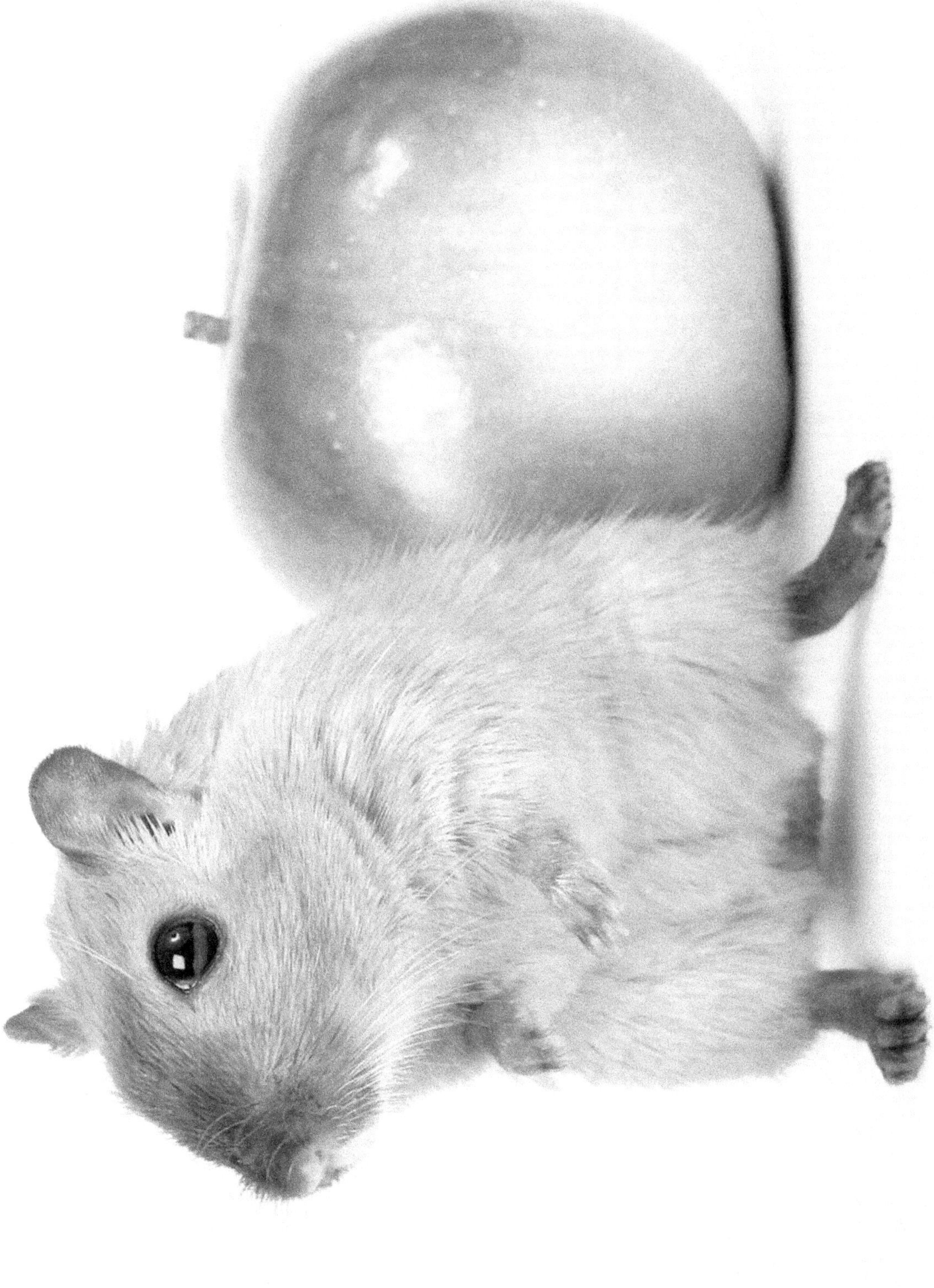

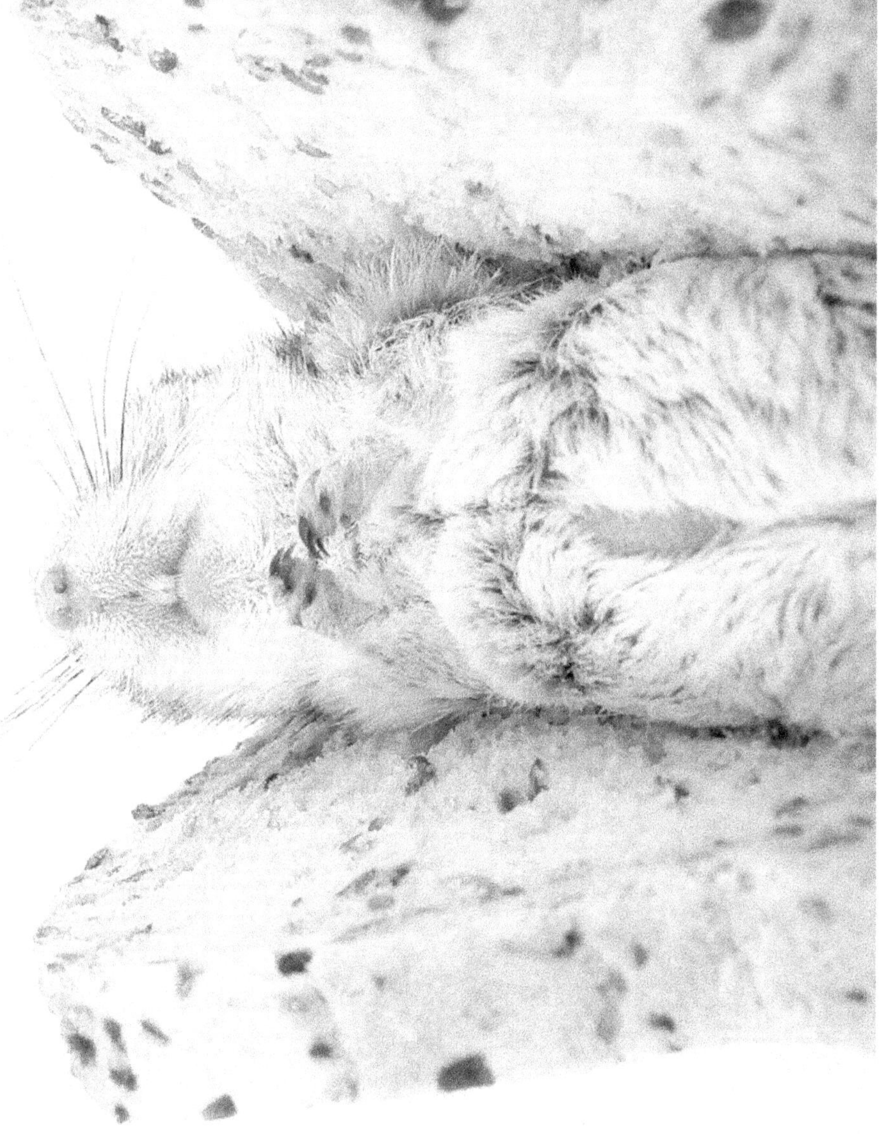

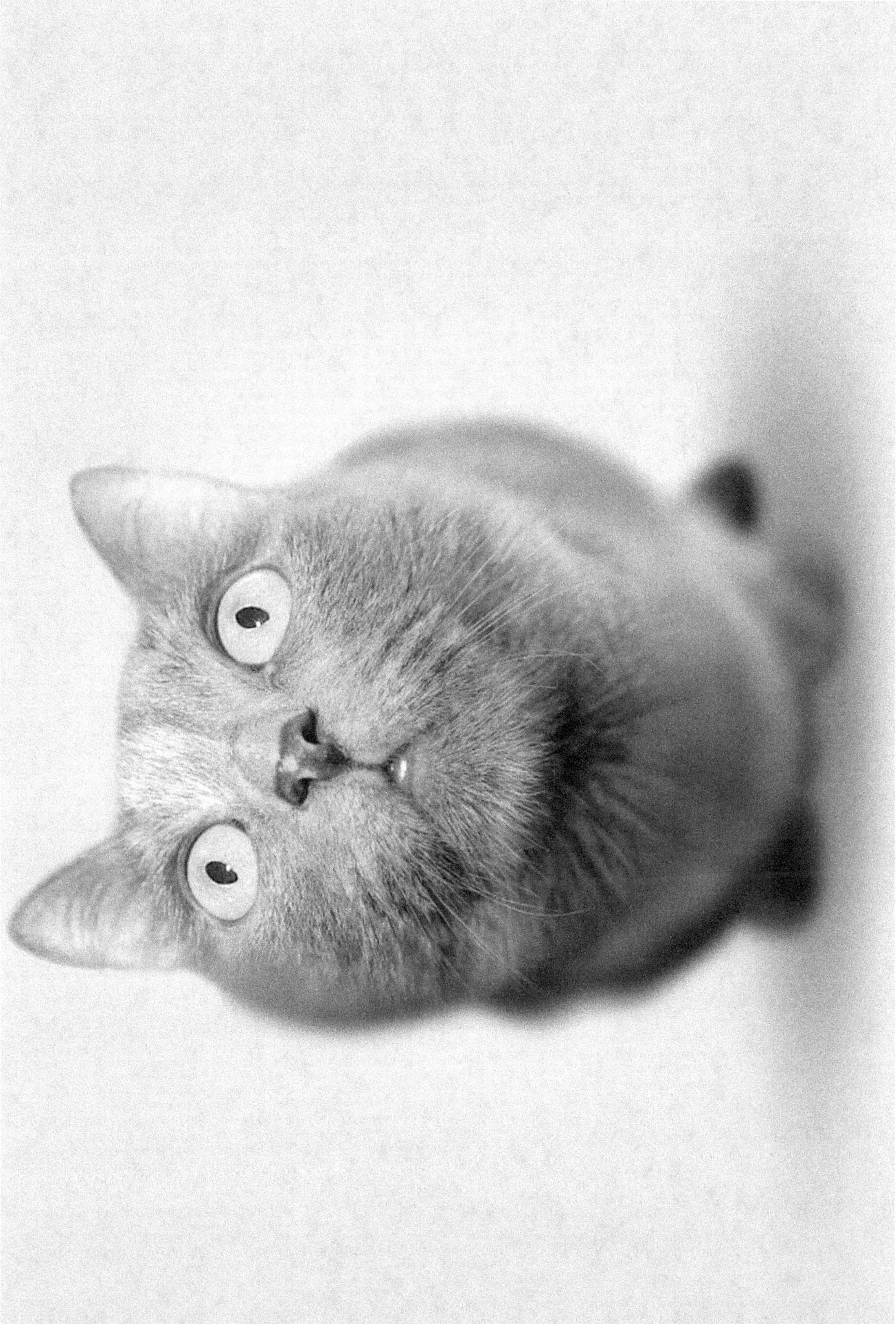

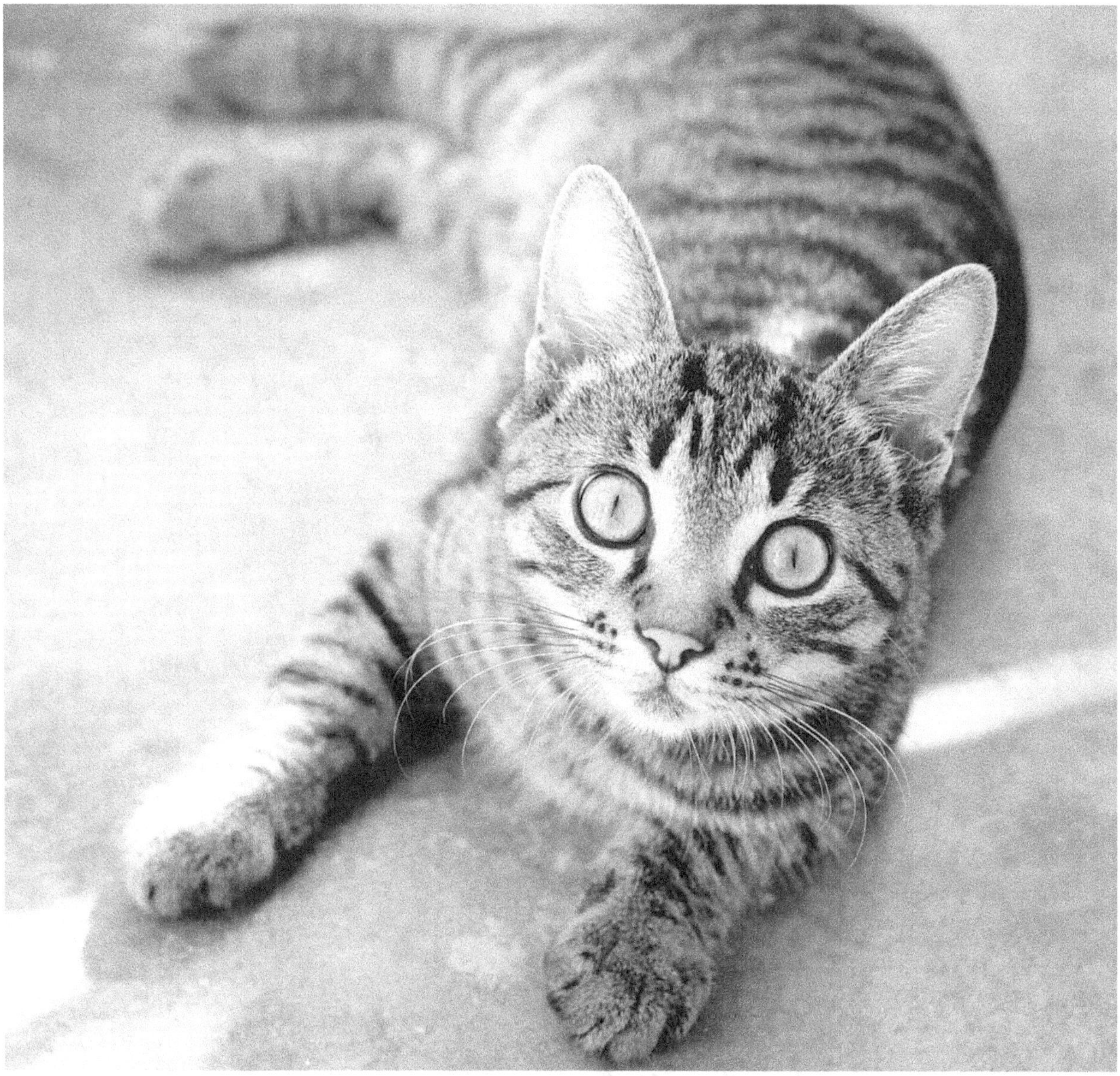

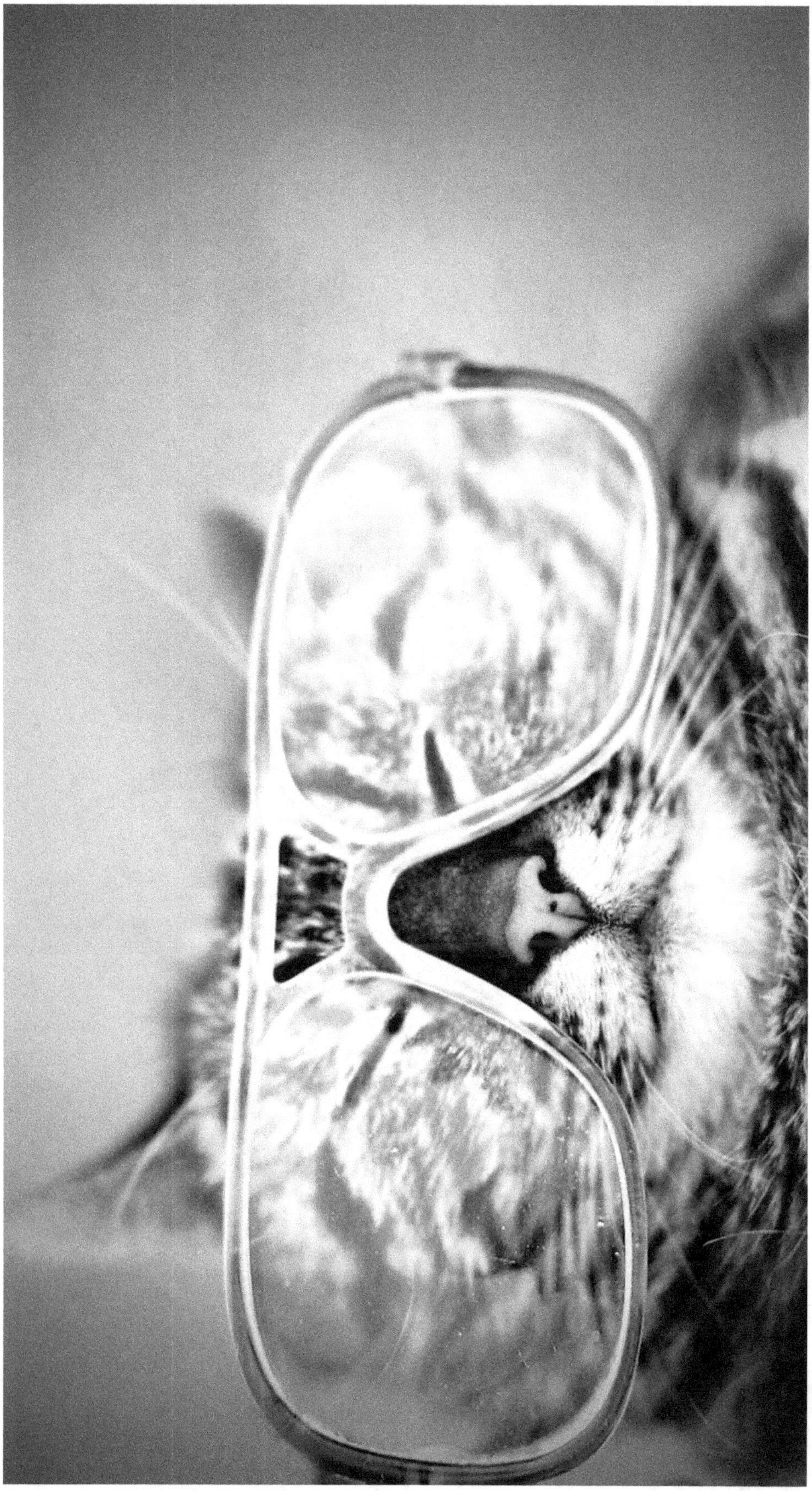

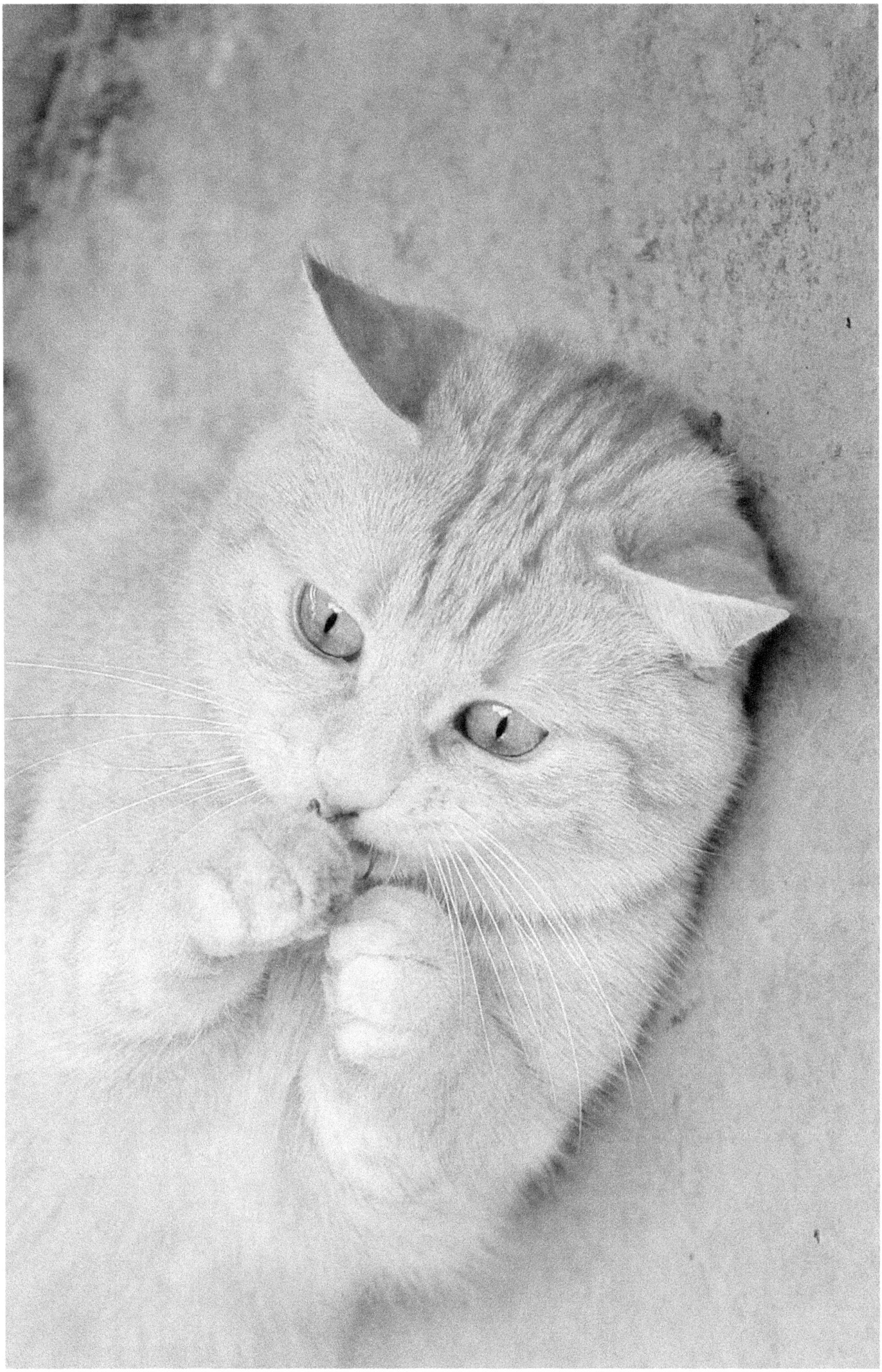

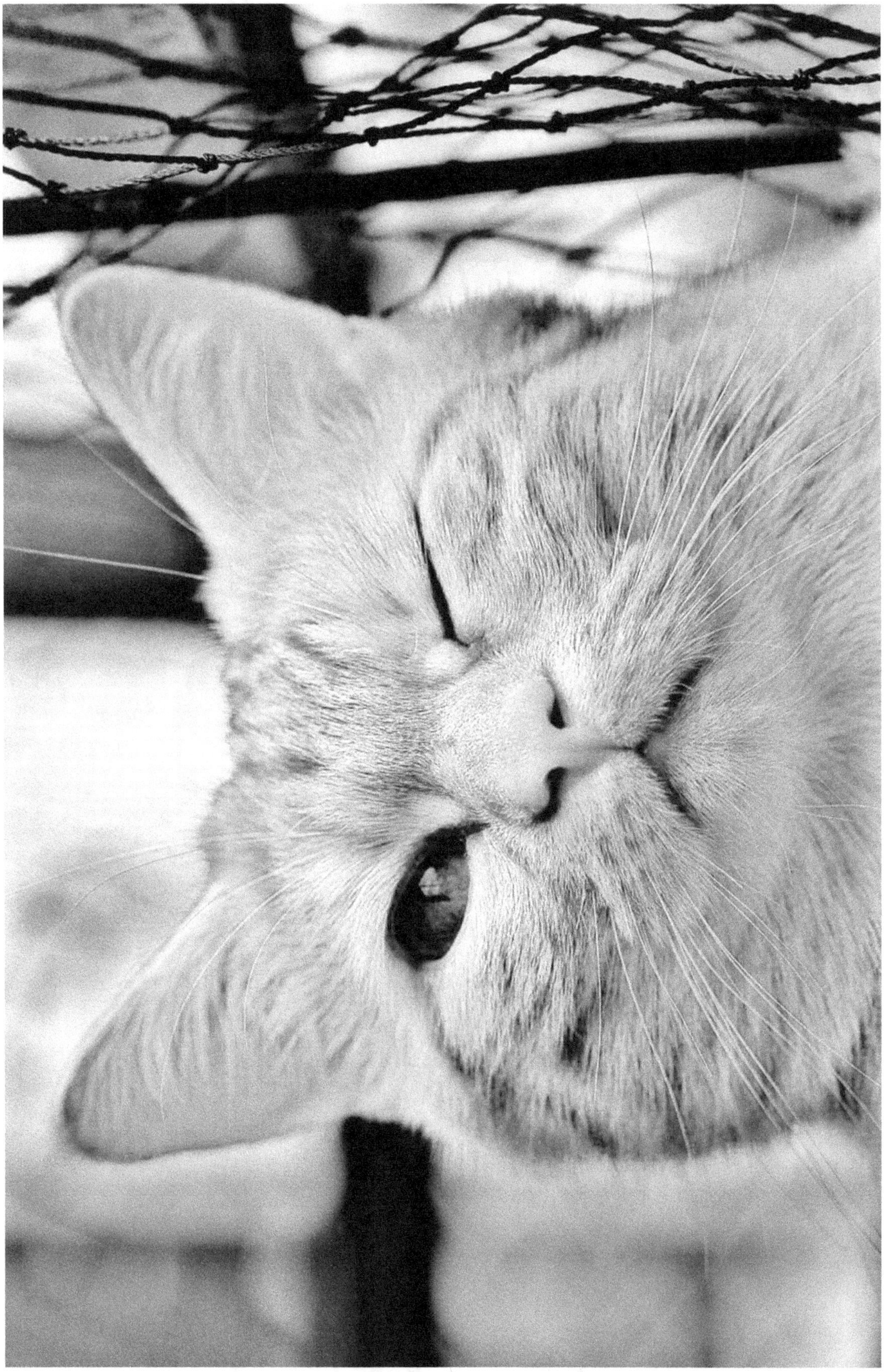

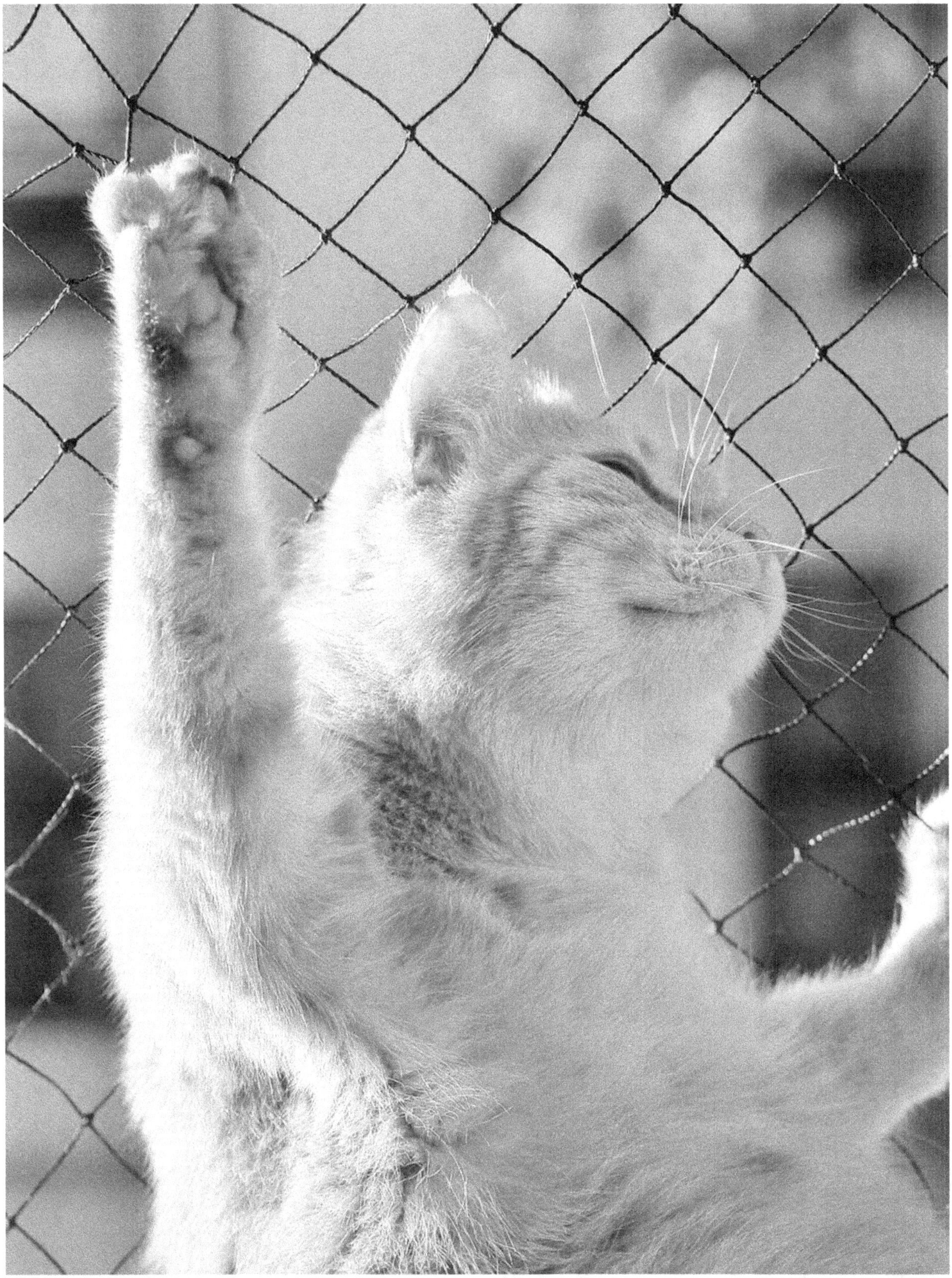

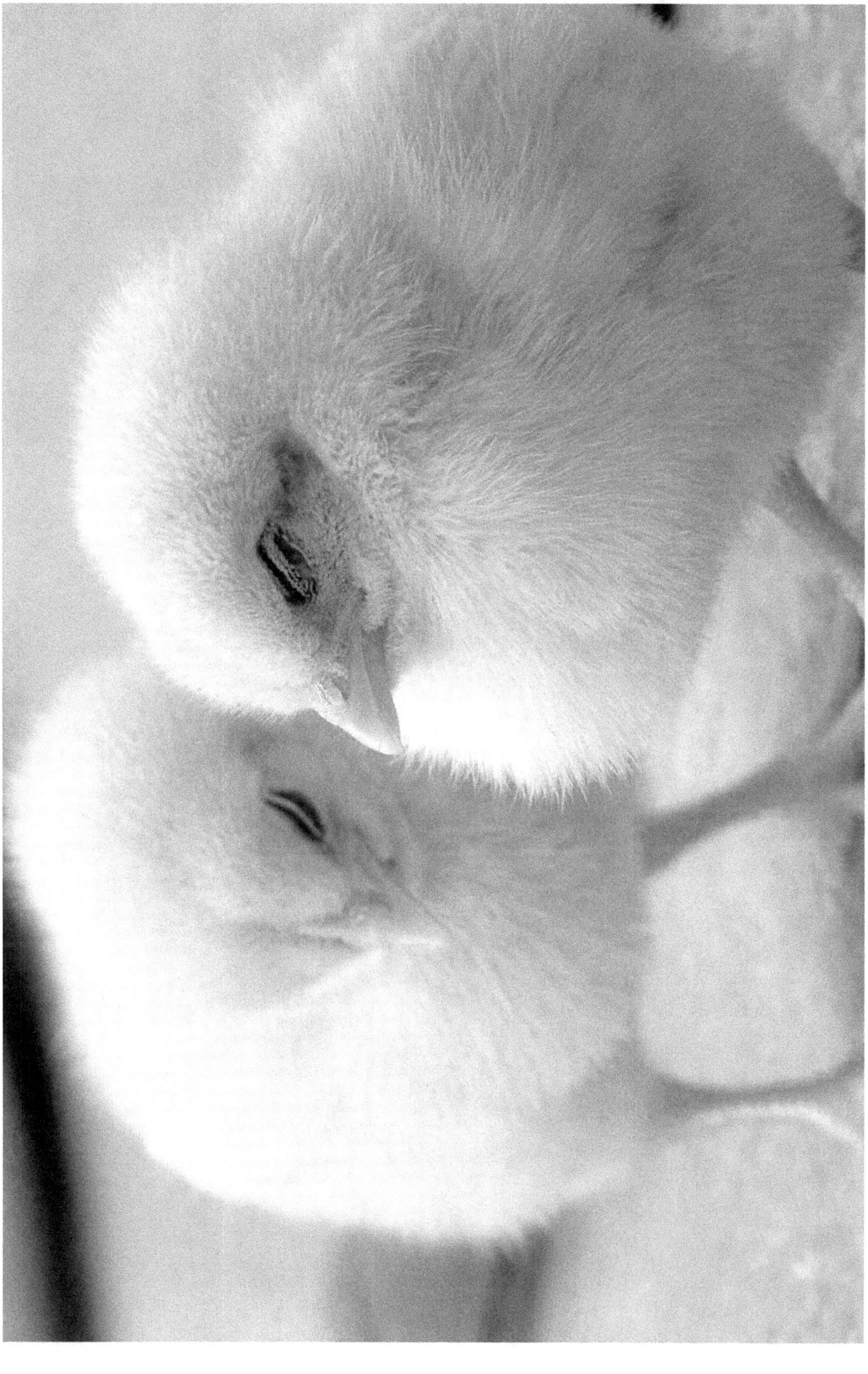

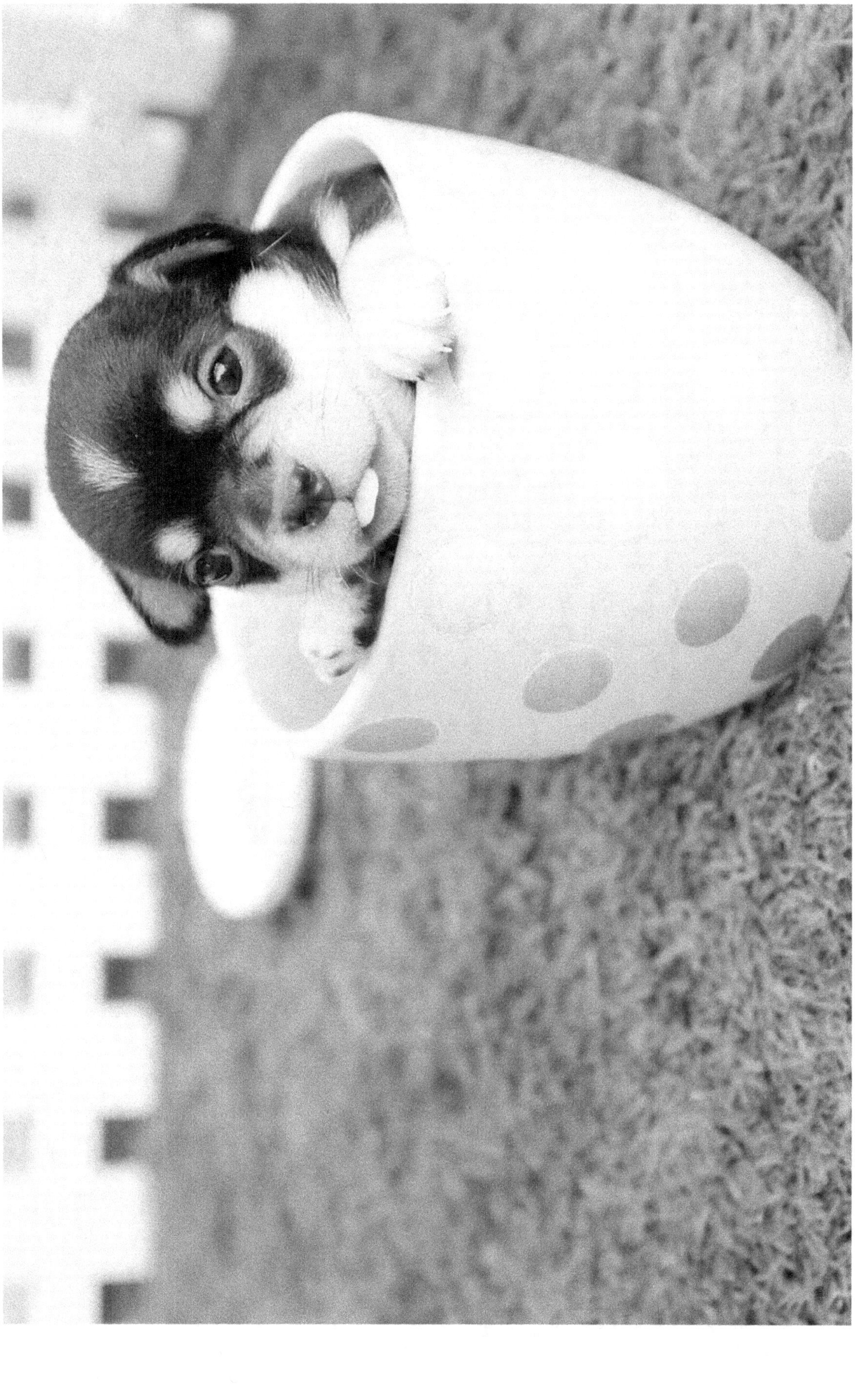

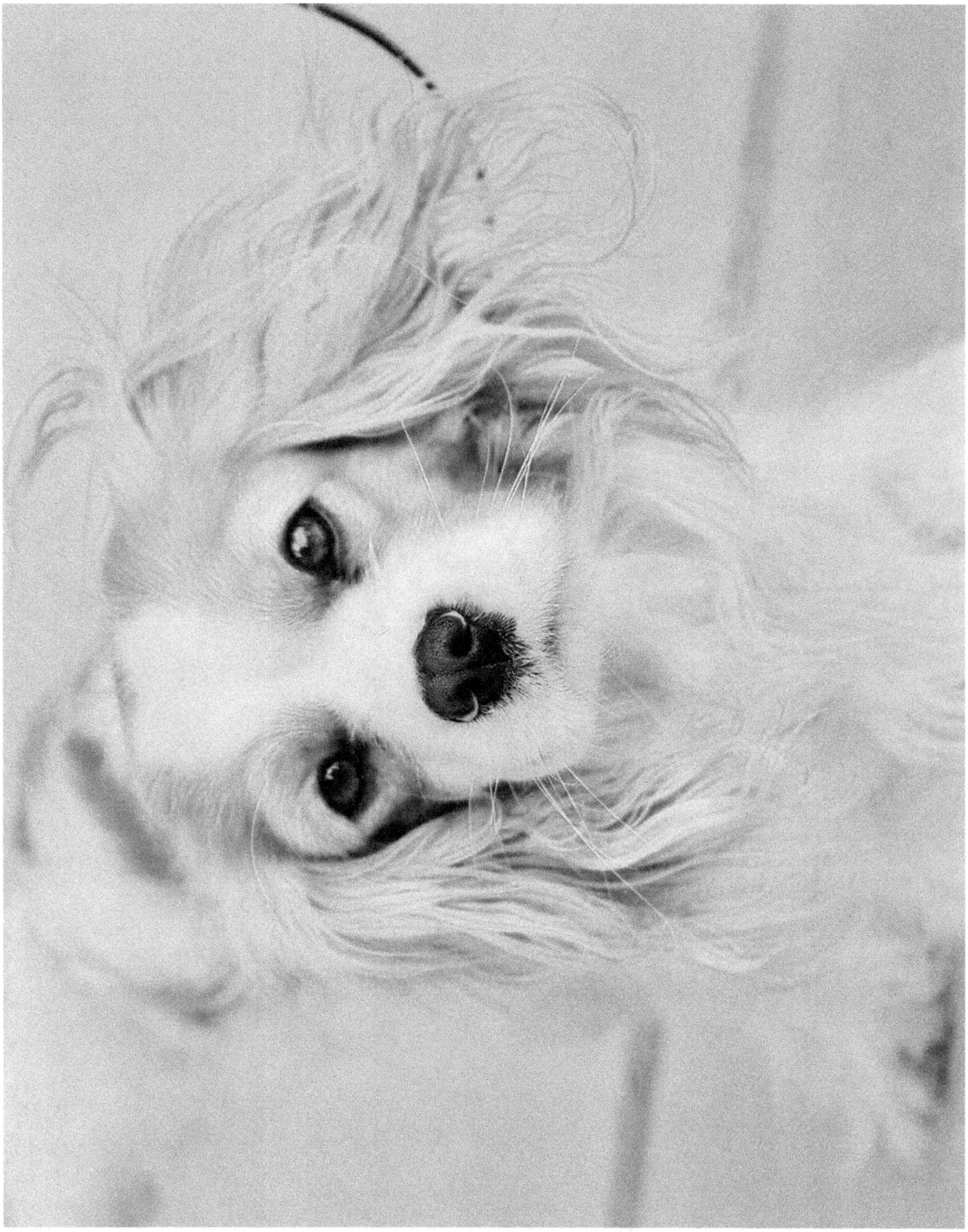

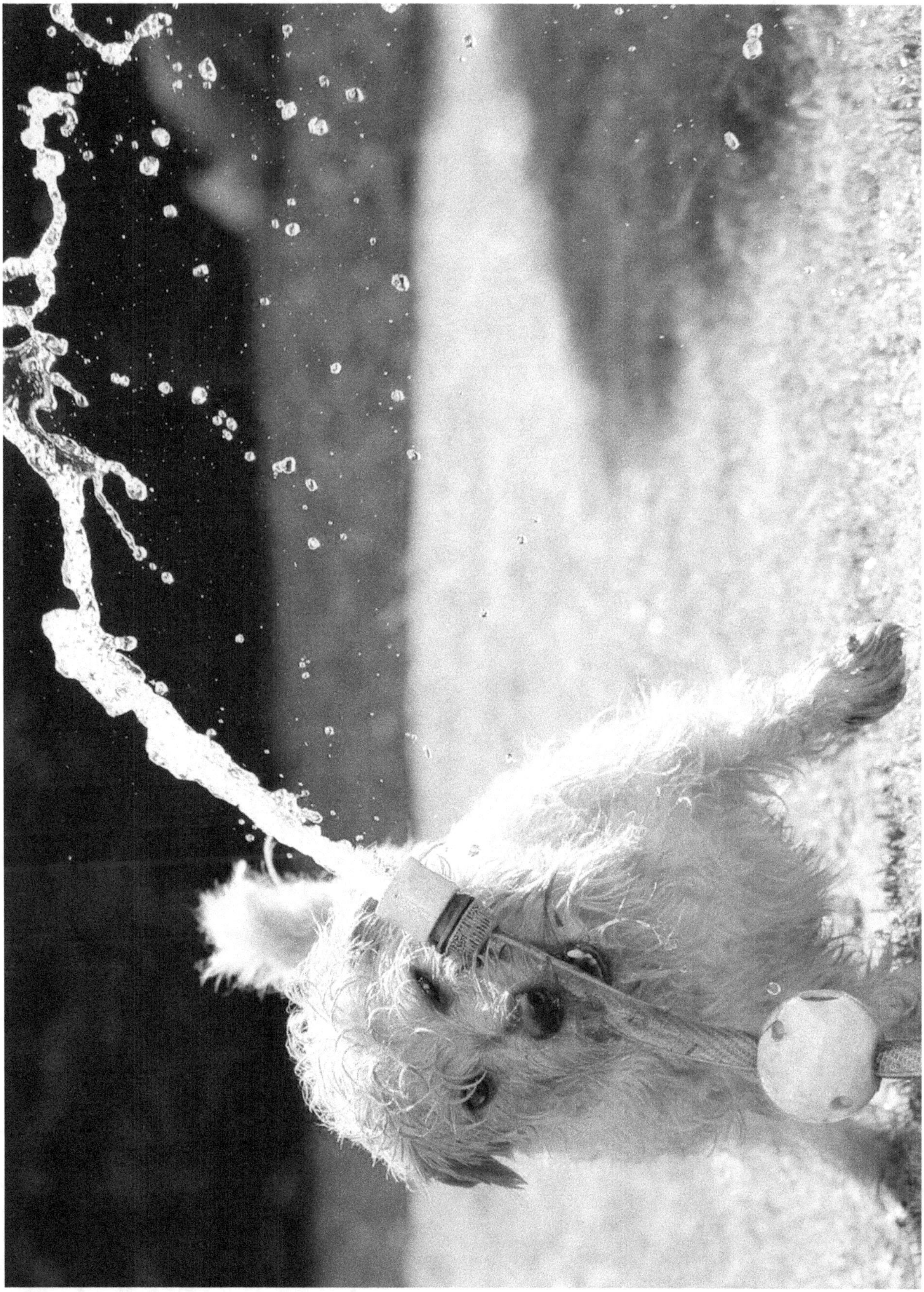

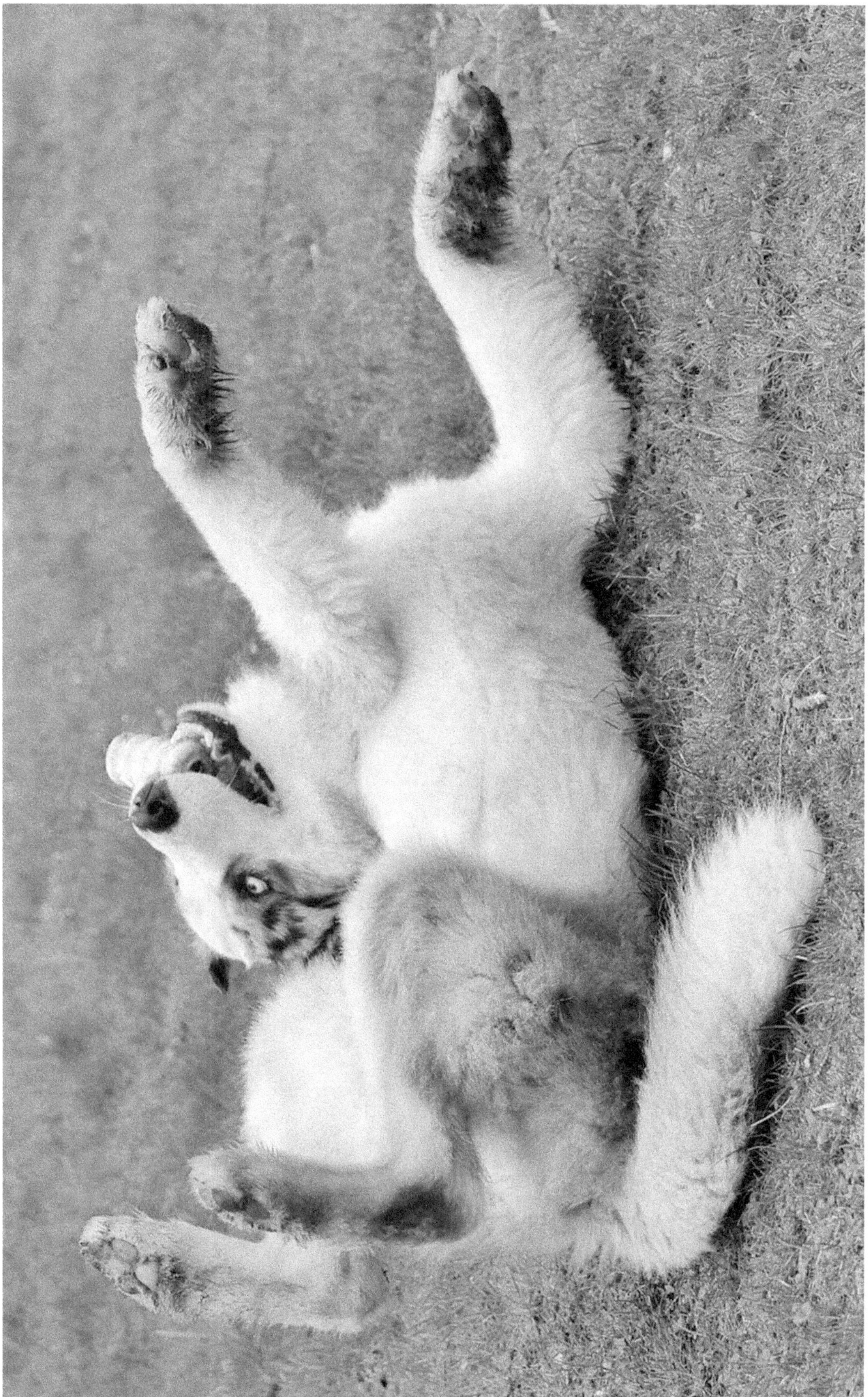

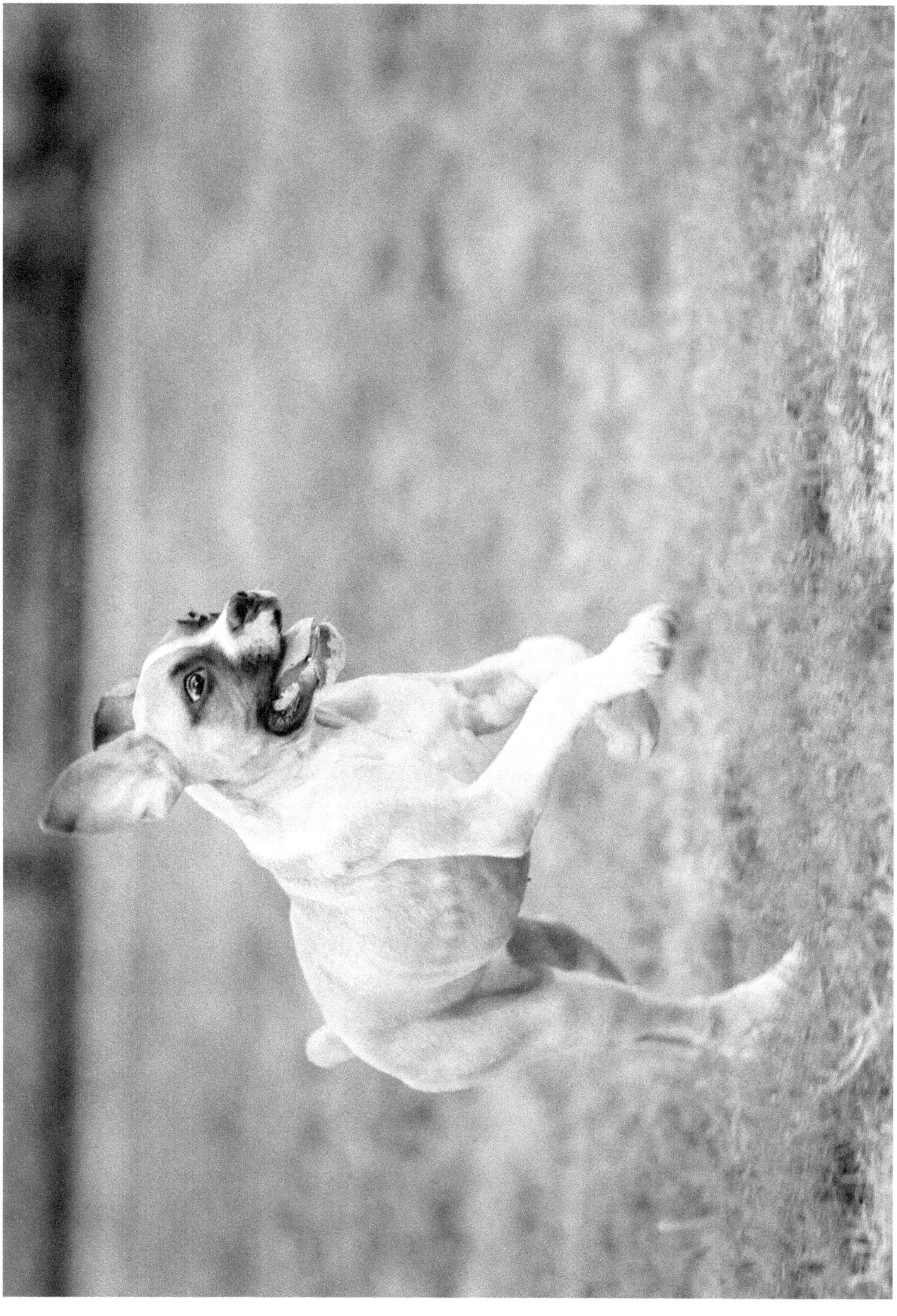

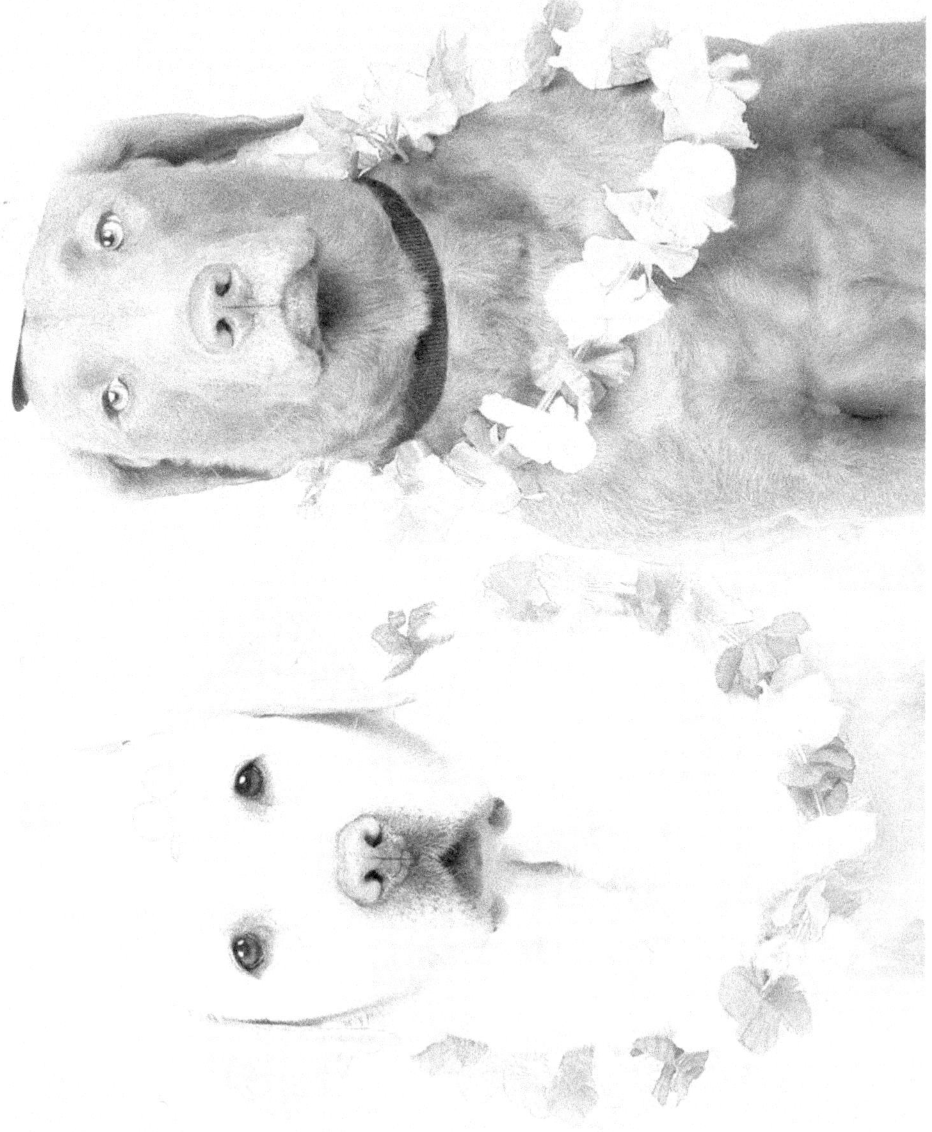

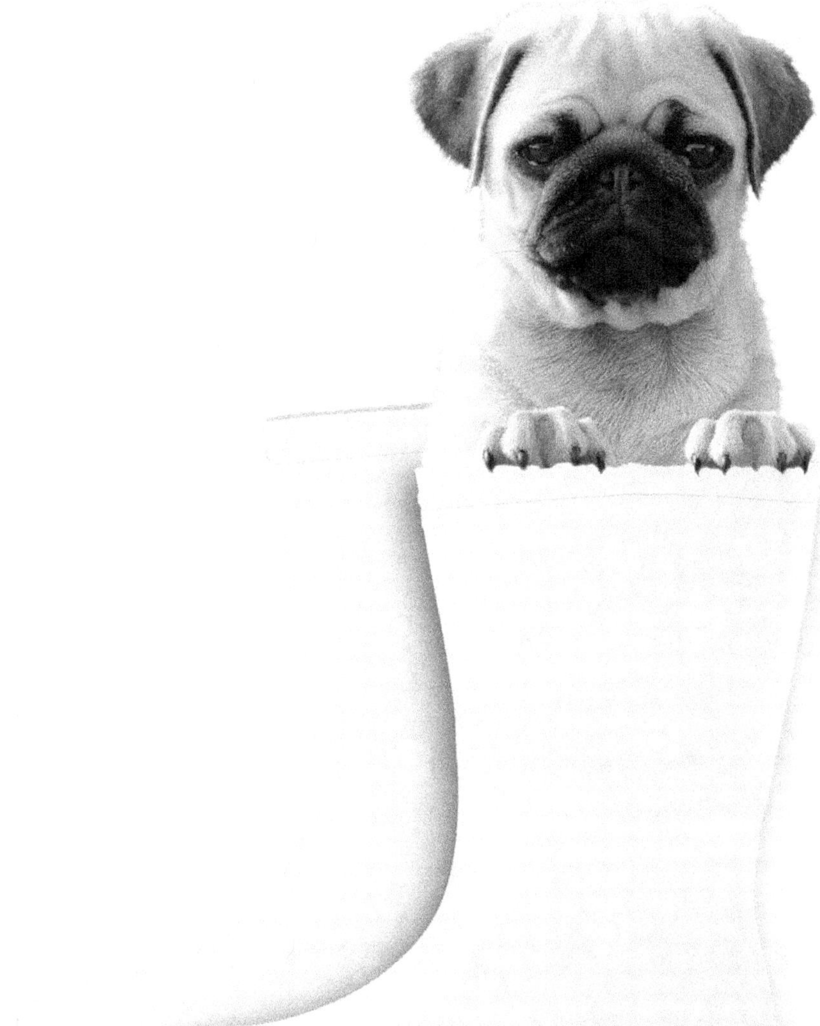

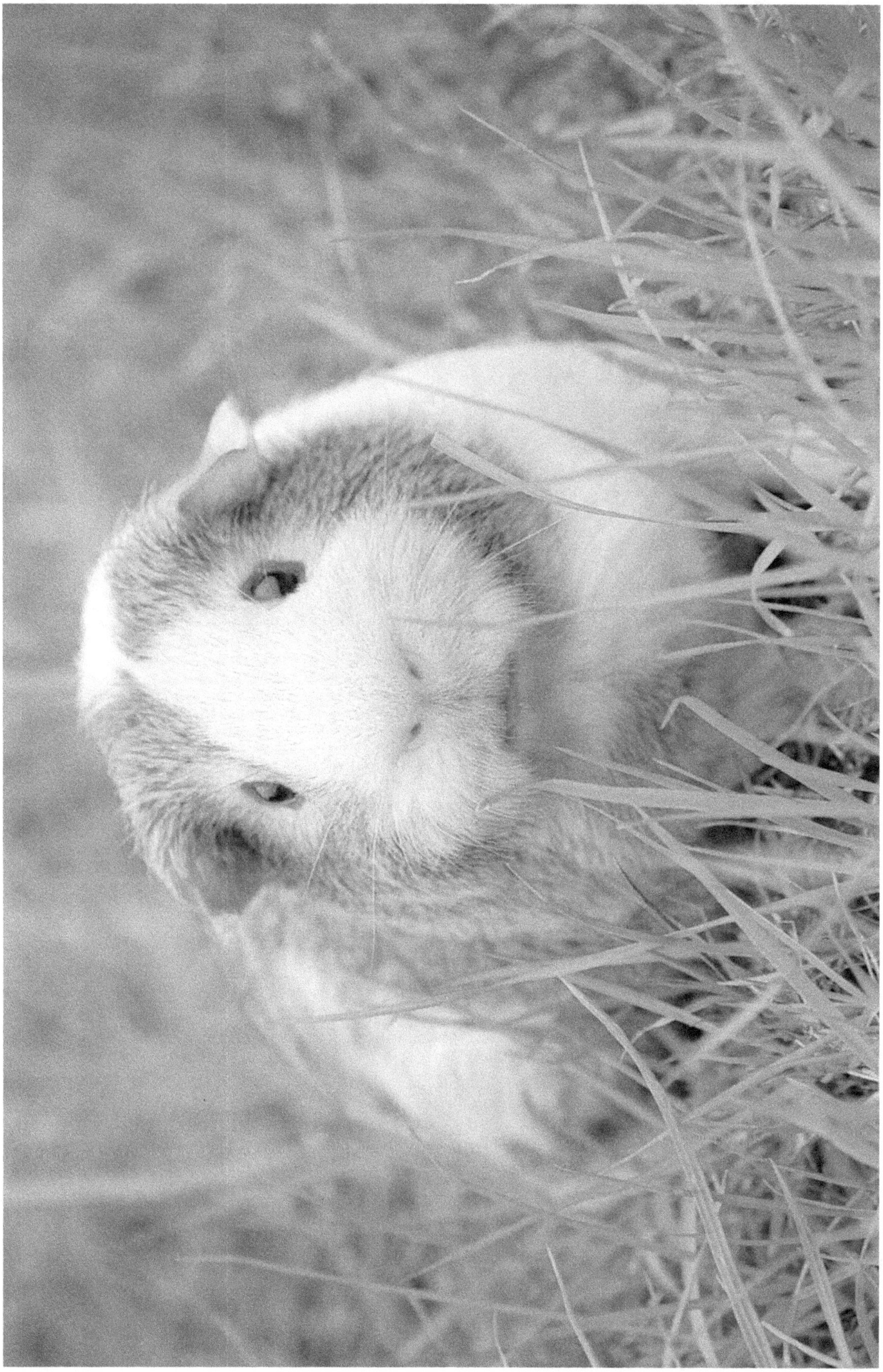

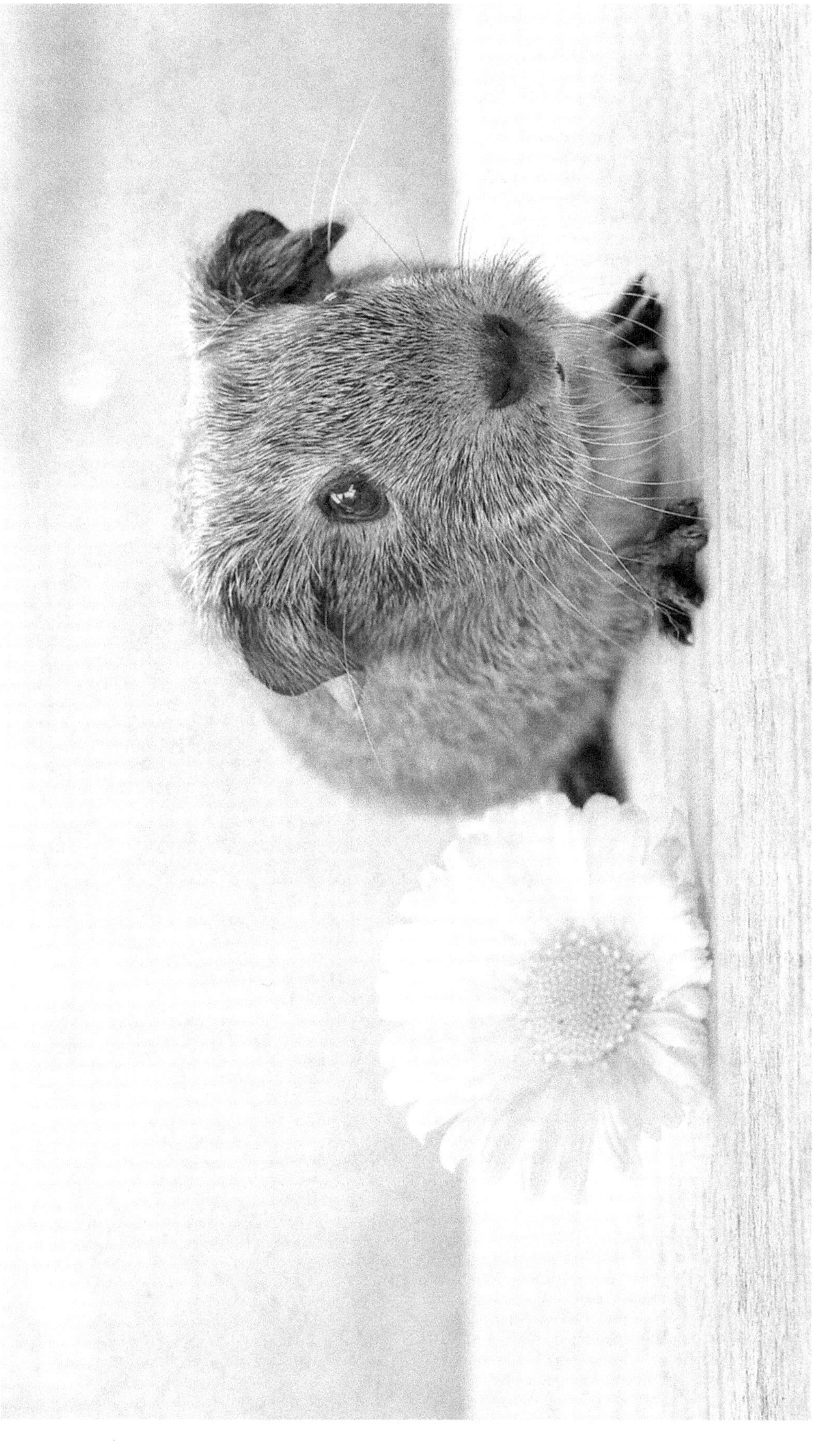

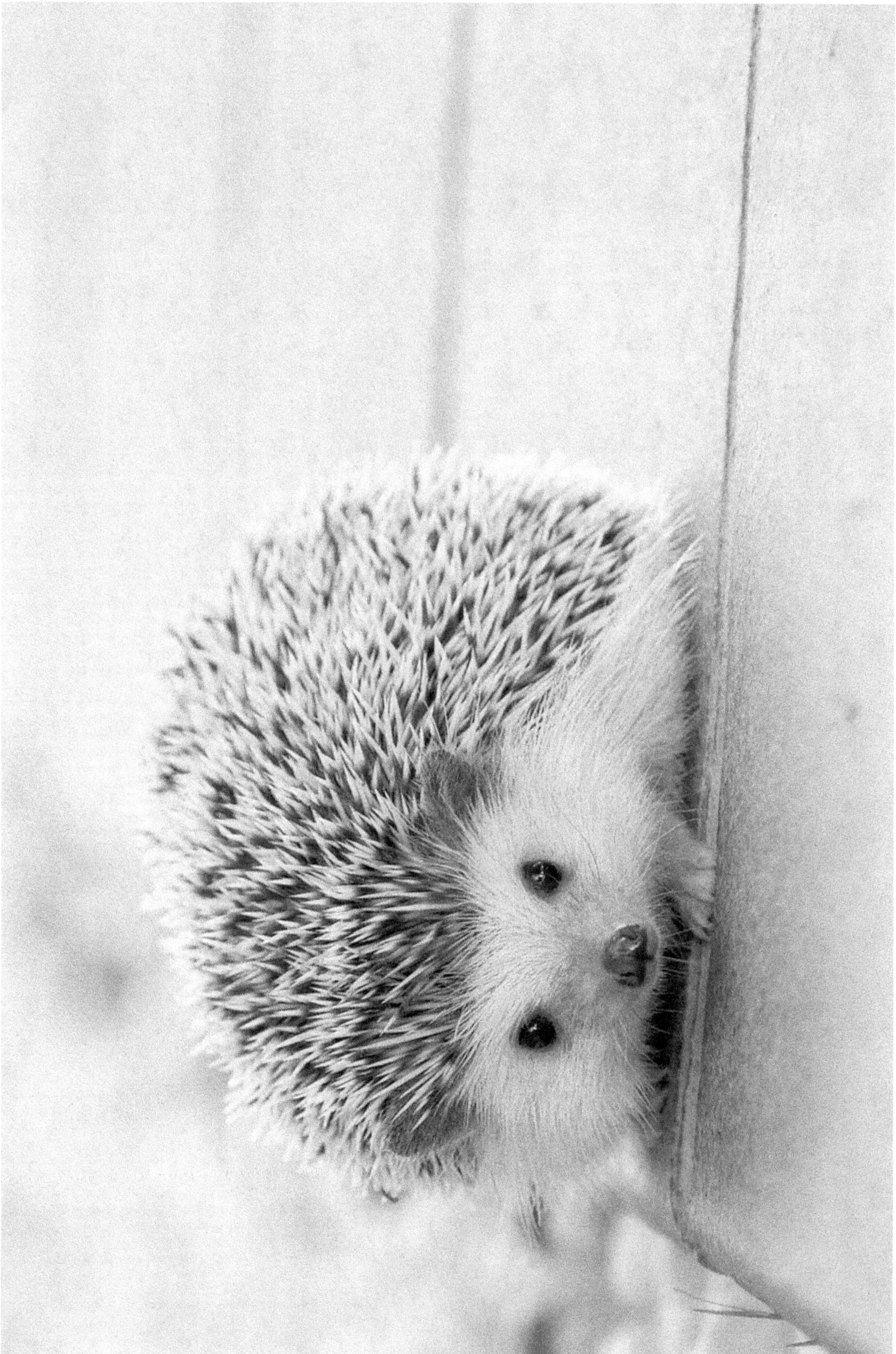

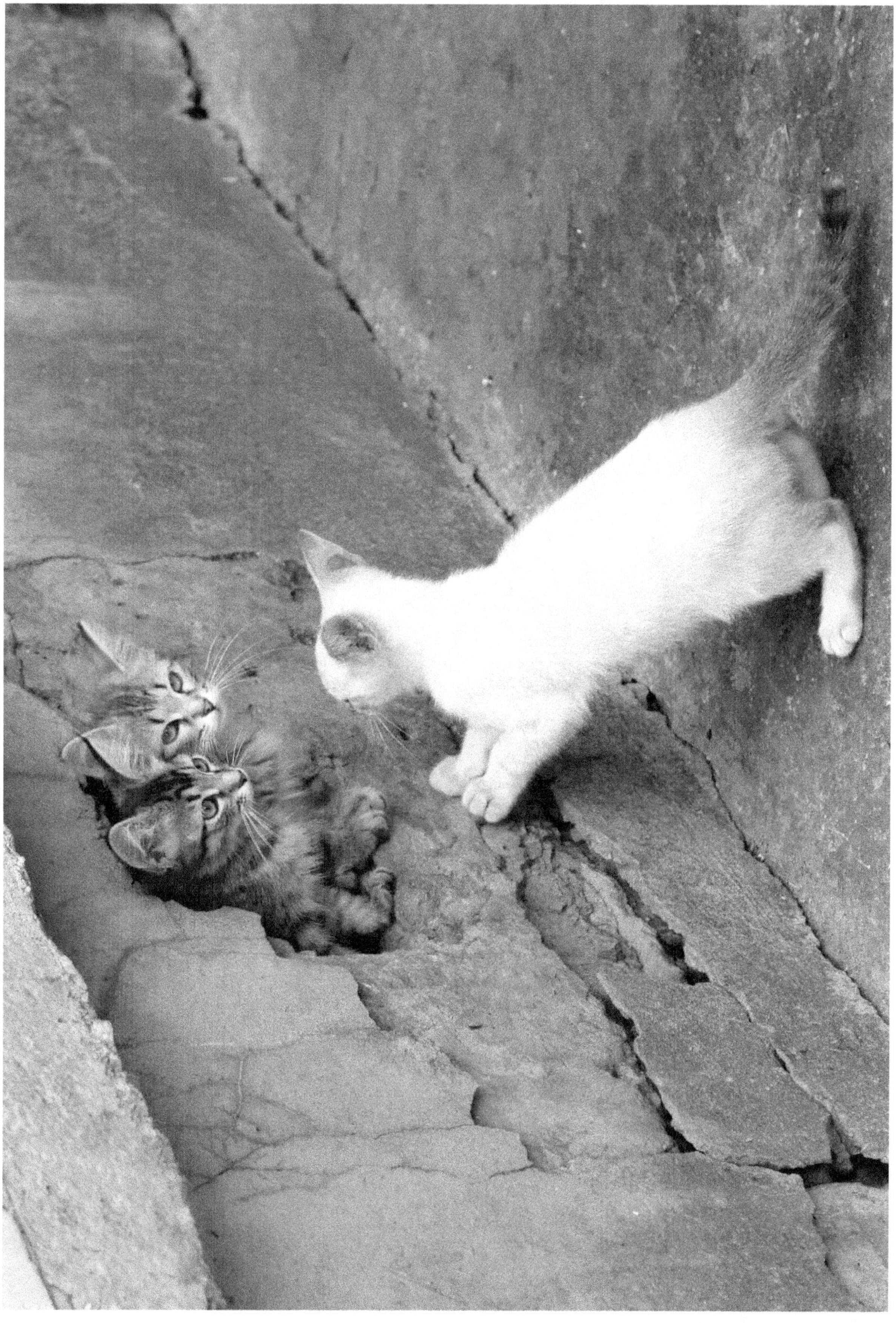

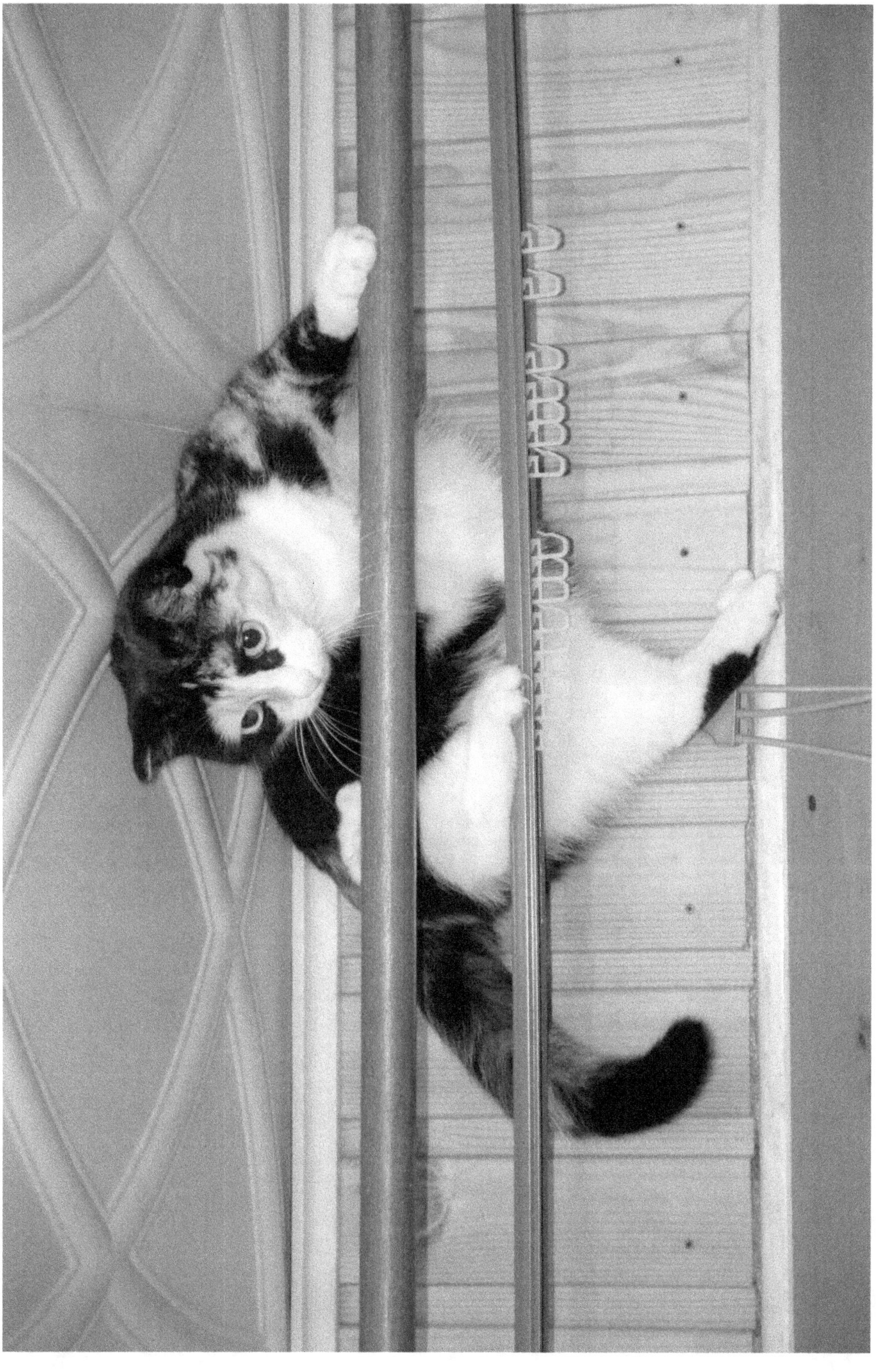

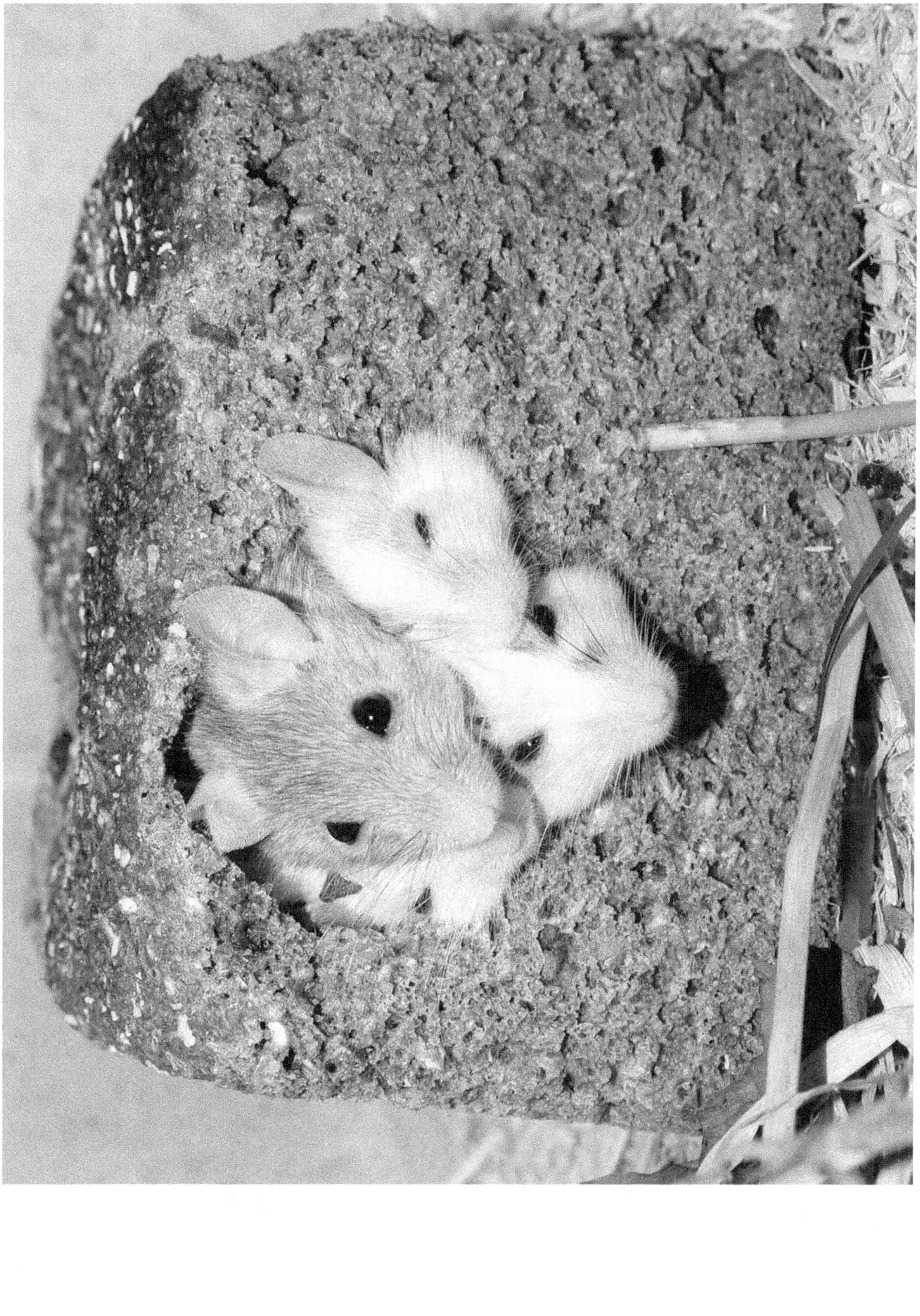

www.ingramcontent.com/pod-product-compliance
Lightning Source LLC
Chambersburg PA
CBHW081125280526
45787CB00007B/2978
9781535040686